Growing Herbs Indoors and Outdoors

With Cooking Recipes Using Fresh Herbs

By: John Dennan

(In conjunction with Kaye Dennan)

ISBN-13 978-1539972280

TABLE OF CONTENTS

PUBLISHERS NOTES

your growing conditions and local area that needs to be undertaken in order to get the best from your efforts.

Paperback Edition

INTRODUCTION

Plants have been a source of herbs from since the beginning of time and the Chinese excel in the use of herbs in their cooking. Not only that they also have excellent skills at using herbs for medicinal purposes.

Today common herbs are most known for their culinary uses but that is changing.

There are though, many medicinal applications for herbs as well and as our society turns more and more to herbs and natural medicines for cures herbs have taken on a whole new meaning.

Some of the best tasting foods are flavored with herbs. Diners often wonder how a particular meal tastes so wonderful when often it can purely and simply be the correct addition of herbs. In different cultures the lower classes usually used herbs to flavor the lesser cuts of meat and fish. This way the same cuts could be used for different meals but with quite a different flavor.

I am sure you cook with herbs all the time. It is just part and parcel of our culture and cooking today. What is becoming more and more popular is the fact that we like to cook with and eat fresh herbs on an almost daily basis. This has developed a whole new hobby of people growing their own herb gardens.

Today home gardeners devote whole gardens to growing herbs. Even the family cook can use a lot of herbs and so the gardens are usually quite plentiful. An interesting fact about herbs is that different cultures tend to like different flavors.

In ancient times herbs were used for a lot for medicinal purposes and were traded as a very valuable item. From the desire to have these aromatic and medicinal plants came many trade routes. The demand for herbs opened many doors to different cultures.

With the use of herbs as a medicinal item, people who discovered certain plants made the body feel better, more relaxed or in less pain, often needed to trade goods to be able to procure enough of a certain herb.

Chamomile as so many know, gives a calming effect, whereas most mints can settle an upset stomach. For the longest time, herbs were the only medicines anyone knew about. That stands to reason when you think that even if there were modern medicines available every country had areas that did not have access to modern medicines on a daily basis.

With the onset of new medical practices, the use of herbs became less relied upon. In some countries it even became illegal to practice the use of herbal medicine. Herbs were then often considered substandard. Many people who had relied on herbs for healing were now being accused of witchcraft.

It was not until the 1960's and 1970's that herbs started making a comeback. The use of herbs in the medicinal sense once again started to gain popularity. Today people are realize that many illnesses are better treated with herbs rather than with chemical medicines and homeopathy has taken a strong turn upwards with many wanting to avoid medicine altogether.

Even though there was so much interest in the medicinal herb the use of herbs as a flavoring for food has never waned. Herbs make a delicious additive to stews, salads, egg dishes, smoothies, desserts, in fact almost anything you can think of. For delicious recipes with herbs included you can view a range of my cookbooks for 1, 2 or more people at: http://www.amazon.com/-/e/B00AVQ6KKM

Another aspect of growing herbs that I love is that I can grow them with the children. By doing this they understand that you can grow food and

they also get to smell the herbs and learn so much about growing plants. I let them go out and pick the leaves too as they have learnt what plant is what. They really enjoy that.

Grow Herbs Hydroponically

Did you realize that you can grow herbs hydroponically? With hydroponic growing they grow three times as fast as the traditional methods and are very prolific. The one drawback is that not everything is happy growing hydroponically so it would take a little bit of trial and error, but in saying that most of herbs do grow hydroponically if set up correctly. A very simple hydroponic system in a sealed box would suit most families' herb requirements and it does not take up very much room either.

You can learn all about setting up a DIY hydroponic system in:

Complete Hydroponic Gardening Book

https://www.createspace.com/4453370

BENEFITS OF GROWING HERBS

If you have done any type of cooking to any extent you will have realized how different an herb can make to the taste of your dish. There is no doubt that most dishes taste better with a little salt, but did you realize that another herb that is commonly used in the household, pepper is an herb. Most people do not realize that.

Pepper is a berry from the Piper Nigrum plant. Black and white peppers are made from the same plant. The un-ripened berries are used for the black pepper while the red, ripe ones are used for the white pepper.

Along with the natural herb pepper, many other herbs are used to create culinary masterpieces.

Nutmeg, cloves, and cinnamon are common varieties of herbs used in the kitchen. Sage, oregano, and basil are three more.

As more and more plants were discovered for their pungent flavor, people started making extraordinary dishes. What would a roast beef sandwich be without horseradish? Try making a good breakfast sausage when there is no sage around. Herb bread would just be bread if it were not for the flavorful herbs on top.

The fact that herbs do not have any calories or added salts, fatty acids, cholesterol and other undesirable additives is the reason why so many people now wish to use them for flavoring their dishes. They each have their own unique tastes and flavors and can be used singularly or combined with other herbs to make a new flavor altogether.

When using herbs in cooking, it is important to remember a little goes a long way. Too much can actually distract you from the natural flavor of the food. ***The entire concept of using herbs is to highlight the natural flavors***. Too much can overpower the food and result in a ruined meal.

Have you heard of an herb called STEVIA? Although stevia cannot be sold as a sweetener for foods, it can be used to replace of sugar. One leaf alone can sweeten a glass of lemonade! You can use this herb in sauces or salad dressings instead of sugar to cut down on the calories.

Many of the meat marinades on the market get their flavoring from natural herbs. Other herbs flavor the meat when cooked with them.

- You can use dill with lemon for fish.
- Saffron in your rice is always a good choice
- Putting rosemary on a lamb roast results in a mouth watering treat
- Mint with lamb
- Fennel seeds with pork
- Dill with eggs

With so many different herbs available there is something for every dish you create.

Having herbs in the kitchen is the desire for many cooks, from the novice cook to the master chef. With the right blend of herbs you can make meat rubs, soup and stew bases, flavor your tea or even create a new flavor of coffee.

LOCATION OF AN HERB GARDEN

Most people grow herbs so that they can pick them either for culinary use or for medicinal purposes. Today more and more people are learning to cook with herbs and more and more people are using natural remedies for a variety of reasons.

Few actually grow herbs purely for their fragrance which is in most cases very pleasant indeed.

Given that herbs are plants that are used regularly for various reasons it seems practical that they are grown where they are accessible most hours of the day.

I like to have a herb garden that looks good but most importantly it needs to be accessible in most weathers.

Given that, there are a number of things to consider when you decide to plant an herb garden.

Because most of the plants in this garden are going to be used in the kitchen the best place to plant them, if possible would be near the kitchen.

Firstly though, you need to decide if you going to grow your plants in the garden or if you are going to have **a series of potted herbs**.

Also, if you are going to plant in the garden, where in the garden are you going to grow them or are you going to **create a new bed**.

What gardeners have been finding very successful are **the raised bed gardens**. These can be made from purchased frames of wood or corrugated iron, or you can make your own from materials that you have around the house.

If you are going to put them in the garden then I believe it is best if you can to choose a position close to the kitchen or back door, or at least for some of the plants. If you want to have the fresh herbs available for cooking easy access is always a key role in how many of them actually make it to the stewing pot. When the herbs are within a few steps of the kitchen you are more likely to run out and pick a few stems to use. If you have to go all the way to the back of the yard, you may not feel so inclined to add that particular flavoring to your dish.

Again, if growing in the garden you need to remember that originally herbs were considered weeds so you should keep in mind that many of them will wander and spread rapidly.

A sunny location is a good position for your herb garden and even better still one that gets some shade in the afternoon is even better. Herbs love the sun, but too much might make them wither or sprout up and go to seed quickly. Once an herb goes to seed, it can become woody and in some cases this means it will be pretty useless for you.

On the other hand if you give them too much shade you will end up with spindly little plants that won't have as much flavor or produce lovely fragrant leaves. This is not what you want in an herb garden. Because herbs are plants that you continually pick from you will find that you need strong growth and to get this you do need sun until about 3pm. Morning sun is always best for plants.

Along with having the proper growth, is the essential oils factor that give herbs their wonderful flavor and aroma. In the full sun the plants are able to develop luscious green foliage and intense oils. The flavors will come bursting out when you use them in the kitchen.

The bottom line to a great herb garden is choosing where your garden is going to be. The right one will make all the difference. Choosing the right spot should be the first priority.

SOIL

You will find that because most natural herbs were once weeds, and in some cases still considered as such, they will grow in almost any soil. But you must remember that they are plants that you want to cultivate and as such must be treated accordingly.

Try to use a natural fertilizer if you can. Herbs like to have a more neutral type of soil. Just by adding some dead leaf compost and tilling it under when planting can make the herb garden grow better than ever. A dose of fertilizer every few weeks through the growing season will do wonders. And in fact it is essential if you are growing your herbs in pots.

The better quality of the soil, the better your herb garden will grow. However, most herbs will grow anywhere. As a matter of fact, you may find that you will have to trim some herbs back quite severely if you are not using a lot of them, such as mint which, it seems, spreads as soon as you turn your back.

One of the reasons gardeners don't succeed with herbs is because they are too kind to them. Because they are so keen to have good results so that they can use them in their cooking, they buy the best growing mix and spoil them rotten. Unfortunately, this is not the best way to go. Just keep it simple, and fertilize occasionally, and mulch so that they do not dry out.

John Dennan

WHAT TO GROW

One problem many new gardeners face is what to plant and what not to plant. It is not advisable to try every herb when you first start out.

There are three different kinds of herbs:

1)   **Evergreen:** these particular herbs require you prune them back at least once a year. You can do it more often, and hopefully you are cutting them for the kitchen If you give them a strong pruning leave them for a few weeks before you start picking again. When pruning cut back to form a bowl shape so that the sun can get down into the centre of the plant. You will want to remove any old growth so the new growth can benefit from the sunlight and not be crowded.

2)   **Herbaceous:** these will die back come winter unless you live in a warm climate where they will struggle on through the winter, and then

grow back in the spring. All you have to do is chop them back when they have died back, leaving a few leaves from which join the new shoots will start. These herbs are also great for container growing, especially the mint varieties. In fact, when growing mint it can be a good idea to plant it in a pot because it spreads like crazy and will take over your whole garden, and not only that any roots left behind will regenerate. Even if you want it in the herb garden it is not a bad idea to plant into a pot, then plant the pot in the soil so that it helps contain the roots.

3)   **Annuals:** Annual herbs need to be planted every year. You will not be able to winter these herbs unless you take them indoors. Even when you do take the best care of them they often still die off.

The best way to enjoy and develop your culinary garden is to choose four or five hardy varieties of an herb you know you will use in the kitchen. This will allow you to get started with the basics of growing an herb garden. It is a great experience which you will be able to enjoy year round.

Some of the more hardy varieties include basil, parsley, oregano, and mint, which funnily enough are some of the most popular anyway. Most herbs are hardy enough to be grown anywhere in the country but there are some which are only going to grow in the more tropical climates. You should check the hardiness zones of the plants you want to grow before you purchase them. This can save you from disappointment.

Another easy way to find out what is going to grow is by taking a visit to your local nursery. What they are selling is a sure bet that it will grow in your area.

Of course, you may find that you can grow some herbs inside when it is cold outside but that may be trial and error or again get suggestions from your local nurseryman.

STARTING YOUR SEEDLINGS

Growing an herb garden is not hard at all because as I said they are almost like weed so they don't need much attention.

When you finally decide on a sunny area for the garden, make sure it is tilled up smoothly. The rich dirt can be bolstered with nutrients if you like. A standard garden fertilizer is all you need.

The hardy varieties like the mint family seem to thrive on neglect. It is as though nothing can kill them.

If putting seeds directly into the garden they must not be planted until after the last frost is over. The ground must be warm and ready for growing. If you plant too soon the seeds will only rot and not germinate. The most successful way is to start the seeds indoors. This way there is no chance of the weather turning and having the seeds die.

To start the seeds indoors, it is best to use gardening trays. You can mark each tray (or row) with the seed variety you have planted in them. This makes it easy to know which is which. At an early stage they will all look the same. Trays can be purchased in either a self watering variety or you can maintain a constant watering source for them or you can use plastic containers that have holes punched in the bottom allowing for drainage. Herbs are not really hard to grow you just have to have patience like any gardening that you do.

Personally I like the biodegradable seedling pots that you can plant straight into the soil and which will disintegrate as the plant grows bigger. I find this saves a few steps and I am not disturbing the plant for planting. I just place a number of them in a tray so that I can move them around easily.

You will want to use a sterile medium for starting seeds. This can be as simple as a good potting soil. One that is full of sticks and other debris may still hold contaminates. This is not a good potting soil to start the seeds in.

The soil can be put into the trays for the seeds at about two inches deep. This will allow the new plants to generate a good rooting system. The plant's life is in its roots. You need to make sure the roots will be able to expand.

Watering of a new planting system can be hard. This is why I recommend a self watering system. The soil does not dry out nor does it get too moist.

The moisture stays just right for the seeds to germinate.

Alternatively you can just give them a light spray two or three times a day. It is important not to have the soil too wet or it will rot the seeds.

It helps to have a cover on the seed tray as this keeps the moisture in and stops the top layer drying out. Many of the trays come with lids but if what you are using does not have one you can make one out of plastic wrap. Just make sure to remove the plastic once the plants start appearing.

Caring for your seedlings

There is no need to fertilize the young plants at this point. That will come soon enough. You will want the plants to get stronger and a little bigger.

When the first true leaves have formed, not as they are forming but when they have formed, you can start to remove the excess plants. Try to do this without damaging the roots of the other plants.

Thin the plants to about two inches or more apart. You must remember that natural herbs are actually weeds. The strongest will survive.

The new plants are a little temperamental. You cannot ignore them and expect them to survive. Proper lighting and watering are needed to make them grow.

If you are going to be planting out when the weather is conducive to good growth then you can plant the young seedling out after acclimatizing, but if you have a short growing season you may need to transplant them into containers so they can grow stronger for the outdoors.

The soil you transplant the new herb seedlings into should be light and loose. You will want the roots to be able to breathe and not drown. Proper drainage is necessary when you re-pot the plants, as well. Keep the pots a little on the small side as this will force some growth up top but give a strong root system.

John Dennan

It can take up to two weeks for some of the herb seeds to start germinating. When they do you will see the little sprouts everywhere. Do not try to thin them at this point. You should, however remove the plastic.

One tip you may want to take advantage of is this. The plants were in a warm place while the lid or plastic was on so before removing it completely you may want to remove the lid for a few hours each day, for a couple of days to allow the young plants to acclimate.

This will allow the seedlings to get used to the colder air of the house. It will also keep in some of the extra moisture needed by the plants as they grow.

You must make sure if you start the seeds in the house that the plants are hardened before being transplanted outside. As with some other types of plants it is not always a good idea to transplant the seedlings into a bigger pot before planting out as some do not like to be moved once they have started growing.

The best way to do this is to acclimatize them about two weeks before planting out by putting them outside in the semi shade during the day and bringing them in at night. Then just before you are ready to transplant them, give them direct sunlight. This process will harden up the plant without any due shock.

CHAMOMILE

GROWING HERBS IN CONTAINERS

Some of the very container plants to grow are herbs. Because many of them are basically weeds you will find that they are quite hardy in a potted situation. This is great because it means that you can grow them indoors and extend the growing season by starting them earlier and finishing them later.

When you grow herbs in pots make sure that you do not overwater them. You will need to learn which need more water, such as basil and which can go without for a short period, such as mint. Some of this will depend on your climate as well.

Because the nutrients drain out of a pot you do need to make sure that you give them a light fertilizer every 2 or 3 weeks just to keep feeding the plant and keep the new growth forming.

Take care when choosing your pot for size and material. The picture below shows a ceramic pot and when you live in a hot climate you will most likely find that the ceramic takes too much water from the soil so it is best to use a plastic pot in that instance.

Also as regards the size you need to keep in mind that the plant only has that particular area from which to get its nutrients as it is bound by the pot so make sure pot is large enough for the type of herb you put in it and ensure you fertilize regularly.

A POTTED HERB GARDEN

Once you have chosen your pot fill it nearly to the top with your soil mixture that has some organic compost mixed in then make a hole and plant your seedling, bringing the soil back up to just cover the root ball.Water the container well.

For the first few days put your pot somewhere warm but not in a sunny window. When the plant has had a chance to readjust place the pot where it can get maximum light, preferably sunlight for several hours a day. The position does need to be warm for good growth, but best growth will be when the plant gets several hours of morning sunlight.

It is also possible to grow herbs hydroponically and if you do this you can have fresh herbs for 12 months of the year. There are very good setups that you can buy to grow say 6 or 8 herbs in the one garden which you will allow you to have a small amount of herbs even through the winter months.

PROPAGATING HERBS

The best plants for propagating are usually the ones that form a wooded stem.

Here is a list of herbs that can be propagated from stem cuttings:

- Rosemary
- Myrtle
- Oregano
- Lemon verbena
- Scented Geraniums
- Santolina
- Thyme varieties
- Marjoram
- French tarragon

To propagate you will need:

- Sharp secateurs
- Rooting gel

- Propagating mix
- Small pots
- Stick
- Plastic bottles with the bottoms cut off

How to:

1.   Look for a healthy stem with a little new growth at the top.

2.   All you have to do is cut the stem just below a leaf node making the stem about 5 inches long.

3.   Then cut the lower leaves off and gently scrape the outer bark off for about 1 inch up the stem.

4.   Trim the new growth off the top leaving one set of leaves.

5.   Pop the lower stem into some rooting gel

6.   With a stick push a hole in your potting mix

7.   Plant the cutting into the hole and firm the soil back.

8.   Set up a cover to keep the soil moist such as a plastic drink bottle with the bottom cut off.

9.   Place the pot somewhere in the shade and water each day.

10.   Allow them to shoot and then plant them out.

HERBS IN THE GARDEN

I have listed here most of the very popular herbs and if you are starting out with a new herb collection I would tend to choose some from here first then add more as you become used to growing and using them.

Give consideration to the types of herbs that you will use which of course will depend on the types of food that you enjoy to cook or other purposes to which you will use the herbs.

| BASIL | BAY LAUREL |

CHAMOMILE	**CHIVES**

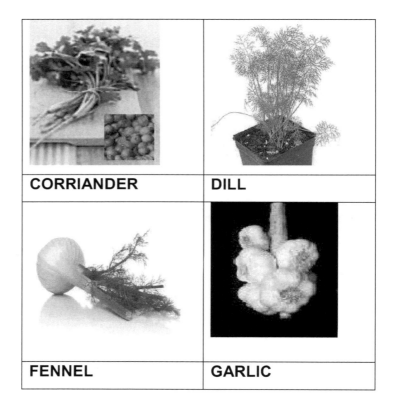

CORRIANDER	**DILL**
FENNEL	**GARLIC**

LEMON BALM	LEMON GRASS
MARJORAM	MINT

OREGANO	CURLY PARLSEY

| ROSEMARY | SAGE |
| STEVIA | TARRAGON |

Basil

Growing basil is relatively easy as it is quite a hardy plant. There are several types and some are more prolific than others, but they are a great additive to salads, pesto and cooked dishes. It loves being picked by the handfuls and as long as you leave some leaves on the stem it will reshoot and grow quite quickly.

Plant basil in a well drained, average quality soil. Although it does like well drained soil, basil does like to be in moist soil so ensure the soil is moist before planting.   If growing it outside, water frequently and lightly, but do dry it out every few days to prevent root rot.   Try to avoid wetting the leaves. As it is a robust plant it does benefit from some light manure every few months.   To help with prolific growth keep the flowers pinched out to encourage more leaf growth.

Bay Laurel

Bay leaves have a very strong but popular flavor when cooking, especially with meat dishes, soups and anywhere that you want that earthy flavor. The bush is attractive and although can grow quite tall, can be trimmed back into a topiary. It is a slow grower but when pruning the leaves can be dried for later use. When growing the bay for eating or cooking it is important that you look for the variety Laurus nobilis because other bay but they are not necessarily edible.

It is best to start from a seedling and it is not too fussy about the soil so that is a help. The bay is shallow rooted and if in a hot dry climate, frequent watering is essential. Bays do last for years and if given care they will produce lovely leaves for your seasonings. Misting the plant is also very helpful in a dry climate.

Prune the plant in the spring and if potted fertilize it gently in spring and mid-summer, but as it is not a fast grower it does not need a lot of fertilizer.

Chamomile

Chamomile, or more specifically, typically the tops gathered in the early stages of flowering, reduces cramping and spastic pain in the bowels and also relieves excessive gas and bloating in the intestines. It is often used to relieve irritable bowel syndrome, nausea, and gastroenteritis (what we usually call stomach flu). Chamomile is also an excellent calming agent, well suited for irritable babies and restless children. Moreover, most children tolerate its taste.

Chamomile is valued as an antimicrobial agent. A German study found that the herb inactivates bacterial toxins.

Chives

Chives are similar to the onion family in that they have a bulbous and multiply easily as well. You can propagate chives by separating the bulbs and replanting. This also helps the system to keep multiplying. Growing from seeds is also very easy so either method may suit your needs.

Generally the chive is an all year round plant, but in the colder climates the leaves may die back and will regenerate again when the warmer weather arrives. Harvest chives from the outside inwards and leave about 2 in of leaf on the bulb.

If you are growing purely for eating, cut off any flowers that appear so that the plants will keep producing leaves only. This is an ideal plant for potting and can be used fresh or cooked. They are great in salads and go well with egg dishes, with baked potato and sour cream and in soups.

Coriander

Coriander is a very popular herb grown to flavor Thai and other Asian dishes. The leaves can be used fresh or cooked and the roots are chopped or ground to flavor cooked dishes. The plant grows best in the cooler months and you will have plenty of coriander for those hot spicy dishes.

In summer the coriander will bolt (go to seed). You can keep the seeds to replant next autumn, but you can also grind the herbs for sauces.

Dill

Dill is a member of the parsley family and is grown for the seed which tend to be on the bitter side and used for pickles. To get a good harvest of seeds it pays to plant in the early spring and the plant will grow to about 3 ft tall. The leaves can be added to vinegar or oil to flavor these over time. The leaves can also be chopped and used in soups, salads and other dishes that would tend to lend to that slightly bitter flavor.

Fennel

Fennel looks a little bit like dill to the untrained eye but they do have different flavors. This plant does not require a lot of attention but it is slow to grow so plant in the early spring.

It has a large bulb-like structure that is the base of the leaf and this is lovely used in stews or chopped finely and mixed through a salad. The bulbous area and the plants and leaves of the fennel can be eaten. The seeds are used as well, often for the essential oil. This is ideal for hydroponics growing or in pots with an average soil and it does like full sun.

Garlic

This is such a popular flavoring that many do not realize it is actually a herb. It is relatively easy to grow and takes about three months before picking. All you need to do is prepare the soil with a little mulch. Gently separate the cloves from a bulb and place each clove in a hole about 1/4 inch deep with the pointed tip facing upwards. Fill back around the clove.

It is best to plant garlic in September in the northern hemisphere and in March in the Southern hemisphere. Shoots will appear in as little as two weeks and you can harvest when the leaves die back.

Lemon Balm

Lemon Balm is a member of the mint family and is grown mainly for a cooking seasoning although it is sometimes use in liqueurs and historically as a medicine. It is very easy to grow, and as mints do, it tends to take over the garden if not kept under control. It does tend to die off in winter but will come back again in spring.

Lemon Grass

Lemon grass is a perennial that grows in clumps. It is a very important herb when doing Thai recipes. The outer leaves of the stalk are tough and not used, but the inner part is soft and flavorsome. This inner part can be chopped and used in curries and stir-fries. Some people even use it to flavor their tea.

Marjoram

This is a perennial herb but often grown as an annual for its fragrant foliage. It is relatively easy to grow in moderate soil and the foliage is used in dressings and meat dishes. It is the Sweet Marjoram that is most popular in the kitchen. It can be grown in the garden, in pots or as a hydroponics plant. It does like rich soil so tend to the soil before planting with compost and fertilizers. As many of the herbs do, it does like full sun.

Mint (s)

There are several mints and they are a very popular perennial herb. Peppermint and Spearmint are the popular ones, although others are Apple Mint, Pineapple Mint, Orange Mint, Chocolate Mint and Vietnamese Hot Mint. The plants grow very easily and do not need a lot of care but they love a deep, rich, moist soil. Mint is prone to rust on the leaves and this can be sprayed if necessary.

It the situation is right it will spread rapidly so for this reason many people plant them into pots. The plant sends out suckers and these shoot really quickly. They are used in cooking with vegetables and is beautiful with lamb and sauces made with mint are very popular. Mint leaves are lovely crushed and served with cool drinks.

Mint is ideal for growing with hydroponics.

Oregano

Loved by the Italians this herb is used in pizzas, spaghetti and marinara sauces. It is one of the herbs that does lend itself to a lot of different uses. It goes well with lamb, vegetable soup, sauces and gravies. It likes a light tilled soil and by keeping it picked will encourage lush, busy growth. Oregano does spread like a ground cover but is easy to control by trimming back.

Parsley

An interesting plant and popular for its blood cleansing properties, the parsley is commonly used as a garnish in many restaurants. The two popular varieties are the curly leaf (most commonly used) and the flat leaf. The curly leave has more flavor but they both grow as prolifically as each other. If care is taken with watering the parsley plant and in keeping it picked, it will continue to sprout more leaves on a continual basis. The parsley herb is popular in a wide range of dishes, both cooked and raw. It is lovely chopped through various salads and compliments even the mildest dishes like scrambled eggs. Some people only use the leaves, but if you are cooking the herb, the stems can be used as well and they have a good strong flavor.

Rosemary

Rosemary is a very popular herb when cooking with meat, especially lamb. Because the leaves tend to be a little hard, the herb is often used as a branch rather than just the leaves. If only the leaves are going to be used in cooking it pays to chop them quite finely. It is hardy shrub and will keep on producing for a long time if given the necessary care. The plants can actually grow quite tall and gives off a lovely scent even as a garden plant. Because of this lavender is used for pot pourri, perfumes and other occasions where scent is needed. It can be tied in a small bundle and hung in wardrobes and then leaves a lovely aroma through the clothes.

Sage

Quite a popular herb, it suits being used with rich meats and in gravies. Sage is often used in sausages and tomato sauces as well. It has a peppery taste that is quite popular. It is relatively easy to grow. It is a plant that suits being dried and used at a later time. The best picking time is just prior to flowering. Sage has good medicinal qualities as well.

Stevia

Stevia plants like rich loamy soil and it is best to plant after the frosts. One benefit of growing Stevia is that is a natural insect repellent. This can be quite a help if you are growing a herb garden as keeping the pests at bay is half the problem solved. Harvesting of stevia leaves should be left as late as possible. Depending on your climate the plants may last the winter and if so, the plant could last up to 3 years. Once you have picked your stevia leaves, dry them then crush them and add water when you want to use them.

Tarragon

This perennial herb tends to be used with some of the milder dishes like vegetable soups, cheese dishes, fish and the like. Another popular use of the tarragon branch is to put it in a jar of oil and let the flavor seep into the oil before the oil is used for dressings and cooking. The plant tends to like rich, loamy soil that holds moisture but drains well.

Thyme

It is a popular herb and easy to grow. There are many varieties of thyme with the English thyme being the most popular. There are two very strong varieties: Caribbean thyme and Summer thyme. It is part of the mint family so care needs to be taken that it does not get out of control. It tends to keep quite small and it does have small leaves as well. Thyme is quite a pretty little plant and popular as an ornamental. Thyme is a popular herb and mixes well with other herbs as well. It is not overly strong and tends be used in the milder dishes.

Variations

In searching for pictures to include to show you the various types of herbs it made me realize that I do need to mention the fact that many of the herbs will show in a different way. For example there are a number of herbs that come with a variegated leaf where I have shown a plain green leaf. Also there are different shapes of leaves within a herb type, such as the regular mint and Thai mint.

Be aware of that when you are shopping for your seedlings or seeds as the different leaves will often indicate a slightly different taste and fragrance.

Lavender which is used in homeopathy

PICKING HERBS

If you like cooking there is a good chance you will want to use fresh herbs and when you grow your own you will have them there as and when you want them.

Unlike some other plants you may grow, most herbs benefit from being picked and picked regularly. Some plants will thrive more so by being picked back quite hard, such as basil, mint and chives. This regular picking encourages the plant to sprout more branches and leaves and grow more abundantly.

If for some reason you have not been picking a certain herb in your garden, then when you are out there and collecting something else, give it a quick nip back anyway.

Harvesting

Fresh herbs can be used for cooking or adding to fresh foods such as salads, yoghurt, drinks, or food that you won't be cooking.

Chamomile for example is a very popular herb used to make a tea that is very relaxing.

As you harvest for the kitchen this allows the plants to keep producing during the growing season.

At the end of the growing season you will want to harvest and prepare your herbs for winter use.

KEEPING HERBS FOR WINTER USE

When you harvest for the winter months you must make sure you gather all you will need. You may even have to slow down picking for a few weeks to allow some extra growth for your winter harvest. Or, alternatively if you know you are going to be keeping herbs over winter then you can plant extra. You will want to make sure before you store the herbs they are dried completely.

There are several ways to keep herbs through the winter period. Of course, none of them will mean that the herbs are fresh, but they will be perfect for cooking.

Drying herbs

You must first gather the herbs you are going to dry. It is best to cut **longer stems** than a lot of short ones. You are going to hang the herbs upside down in a well ventilated area. You do not want to hang them in bright sunlight. Although the sunlight will make the herbs grow wonderfully, the light can cause the herbs to lose some of their potency when drying.

Hanging herbs

When you have cut four or five long (8 to 10 inches) stems off your herb plant, you need to shake them off gently. This will ensure there are no insects on the leaves or branches.

Strip off any dead or diseased leaves. Make sure you also strip about the last three inches of the stem. You need to tie the cuttings together at the bare end. You can use string or even a rubber band if you wish.

An important point at this stage is to make sure that the herbs are totally dry before you tie to prevent them going moldy due to moisture.

By now you should have collected some paper bags about 10 inches long and made some ventilation holes in them. After you have tied the herbs into bundles, insert the stems into a brown paper bag that has had a small hole made at the bottom, bringing the bag down over the branches. Tie the open end of the bag. You can then hang the entire package upside down by using the same string you had tied everything together with. Hang them in a dry environment with plenty of air flow. Don't forget to label the bags so that you know what is in them because they can look much the same when dried.

Keep a close eye on the herbs as they dry. You do not want them to become moldy. Just be patient. Once they are completely dried, you can prepare them for storage.

Air drying herbs

You can also air dry the herbs. Air drying is simply spreading the leaves of the herbs onto screens so the air can penetrate both sides of the leaf. This will allow the herbs to dry uniformly. It is best to use one screen for each type of herb. You do not want to risk drying your peppermint with the oregano. This could result in some rather strange tasting Italian dishes!

Do not make the mistake of thinking you will not use that much. In the summer when you have a good supply of fresh herbs, you may not realize how much of the herb you use. This is because the plant is constantly growing and replenishing your supply.

Dried herbs are stronger in flavor than the fresh ones. Fresh herbs contain water. The dried herbs contain a more concentrated essential oil. You will find you do not need to use as much of the dried herbs to get the same flavors. Yet with the ability to store your own herbs, you might want to make sure you have enough until next spring. If you do have too much towards the end of the winter season you can always give them away.

There is a misconception that herbs can be oven dried or heated to force dry them. ***This is not the best way to dry your herbs***. The heat can actually release the essential oils which give the herbs their wonderful aroma and flavor. It makes no sense to use a drying system which will prematurely release the very thing which makes the herbs so desirable.

The important thing to remember from all of this is to make sure the herbs are kept in a warm, dry, and ventilated area while you are waiting for them to dry.

Storing dried herbs

Firstly, realize that if herbs are not totally dry when being stored then there is a possibility that mildew will form. This is why some people will still freeze the dried herbs.

There are times when you think the herbs are dry but later you find they are mildewing in the jars. This means moisture still existed in the leaves. When you freeze the dried herbs, if there is any moisture, it will not affect the herbs.

Many times you will find it easy to store dried herbs in containers. The best container is one which does not let in light. You can find many apothecary jars with tight fitting lids or even rubber seals. These are the perfect storage containers. With a dark colored jar or bottle the light cannot get to the herbs. Making sure the lid seals properly assures no air can get into the herbs causing them to go off.

Storing herbs in oil is also a good way to preserve the flavor. As long as the oil stays fresh you can keep the herbs. Make sure the leaves are dry and insert into an oil filled jar. This will preserve the flavor. If the oil goes bad, which usually happens in six months or so, the herbs must be disposed of. One of the benefits of preserving the herbs in the oil, is you will wind up with an herbal oil which is excellent in cooking.

Depending on how long you want to keep the herbs you may actually use several methods to store your favorite herbs.

Freezing herbs

One method which many people find very simple is freezing. There are two ways to freeze herbs.

1. **The free flow method:** You can collect the fresh leaves and put them on a cookie sheet in the freezer. When the leaves have been frozen completely, just place them in a storage bag, label the bag with the date and contents, and

stick it back in the freezer. Just do not expect the herbs to act or look like fresh when you thaw them. But they will still be good for cooking.

2. **Ice cubes:** Another way to freeze fresh herbs is to fill an ice cube tray with the chopped leaves from the herb plant you desire then fill the tray with water and freeze. When the ice cubes have completely frozen, shake them out and then you can store the loose ice blocks in bags or containers but do ensure that you have labeled. You can then take them out of the freezer one cube at a time to add to stews, soups, and other dishes. This is a great idea for herbs that you like with cold drinks like mint and the like.

COOKING WITH HERBS

There are several tips that are worth noting when using herbs for culinary purposes:

- Using the leaves – add fresh leaves in the last 2 minutes of cooking and that way they will not wilt too much and be tasteless
- Use leaves in fresh salads, such as basil, parsley, mint and coriander – they are delicious
- When cooking delicate dishes like scrambled eggs, use delicate herbs and not too much of them, whereas if you are cooking beef you can afford to use the stronger flavors and more of them
- If you are using mint in salads tear the leaves, do not cut them because they will go black very quickly. Also tear basil leaves. It is best to add herb leaves to salads just before serving
- Until you are familiar with using a particular herb in a particular way err on the side of caution and do not

use too much, you can always increase the amount next time

Any dish can be enhanced with the use of herbs. Their natural fragrance and flavor just add that perfect blend to make a meal complete.

- Herbs like oregano and basil are the base of many Italian dishes.
- Cilantro and Cumin are what make Mexican dishes taste so authentic.
- More exotic spices like allspice and ginger can add beauty to the kitchen as well as tasteful treats to the mouth.

There is a difference between using fresh and dried herbs in cooking. The fresh herbs add a delicate flavor. The essential oil is not as concentrated as it is in the dried herbs. The general rule of thumb when using dried herbs is 1 teaspoon dried to 1 tablespoon fresh herbs.

Here are some herbs and their uses in cooking

NAME	USE	TYPE
Angelica	Jellies, Drinks, Candies	B
Basil	Sauces, Casseroles, Salads	A
Bay Laurel	Soups, Sauces, Seafood, Stews	A
Chives	Salads, Soups, Cheeses, Eggs	P
Dill	Soups, Salads, Sauces	A
Fennel	Meats, Fish, Sausage, Salad, Salsa	A
Marjoram	Soups, Sauces, Vegetables	A
Mint(s)	Teas, Jellies, Salads, Salsa	P
Oregano	Italian foods, Sauces	P
Parsley	Salads, Garnish, Sauces, Eggs	A
Rosemary	Meats, Sauces, Lamb	A
Sage	Sausages, Fish, Casseroles	P
Savory	Stuffings	P
Stevia	Beverages, Sauces, Soups	P
Tarragon	Salads, Fish, Meats	P
Thyme	Stuffings, Soups, Meats	P

TYPE: A = annual;   B = Biannual; P = Perennial

Don't limit yourself to this list.

Experiment, discover, experience!

RECIPES

A mortar and pestle are a great way to blend flavors. The mere breaking of the leaves allows the oils to be released and this is what you need to get those concentrated flavors.

Refer to Resources for more links to recipes and other information.

TACO SEASONING

2 teaspoons beef or chicken bouillon (use powder or granules)

4 teaspoons cornstarch

1/4 cup dried onion flakes

4 tablespoons chili powder

3 teaspoons ground cumin

3 teaspoons dried garlic flakes

2 teaspoons dried hot pepper flakes (optional)

1-1/2 teaspoons dried oregano

Mix this all together. Store in a jar or storage bag until ready for use. Three tablespoons of this mixture added to one pound of ground beef plus one cup of water. Simmer until desired consistency. Salt and Pepper to taste.

PESTO

2 cups fresh Basil leaves

½ cup fresh Parmesan (grated)

½ cup virgin olive oil

1/3 cup pine nuts

3 cloves garlic

Salt and pepper to taste

Add basil and pine nuts to processor and pulse. Add the garlic and pulse once again. Slowly drizzle in the olive oil while blending. Add the Parmesan cheese and blend until smooth. Add the salt and pepper to taste. Serve over hot pasta.

It is easiest to prepare this in a food processor. You can use a regular blender however you may need to process longer.

CAJUN SPICE

1/4 pound kosher salt

1/2 cup chili powder

1/2 cup paprika

2 tablespoons onion powder

1/3 teaspoon cumin

3/4 teaspoon cayenne pepper

1-1/2 Tbsp dried thyme

2 tablespoons coarsely ground black pepper

2 tablespoons dried basil

2 tablespoons dried oregano

2 tablespoons ground coriander

1/2 teaspoon white pepper

Blend all the ingredients together. Store in an air tight jar or container. This is the recipe you would use to blacken fish or other meats.

John Dennan

ITALIAN SEASONING

4 Tablespoons oregano

4 Tablespoons marjoram

4 Tablespoons thyme

4 Tablespoons basil

2 Tablespoons rosemary

2 Tablespoons savory

Mix well and use as a seasoning in your pasta sauces. This is also great sprinkled on pasta and tossed with a little virgin olive oil. You can make it a meal by adding 1 pound browned Italian sausage, 1 cup Parmesan cheese, and sautéd onions and green bell peppers. Kids love this combination. Make it a treat by adding pepperoni slices.

PERFECT SALT SUBSTITUTE

1 tablespoon ground cayenne pepper

1 tablespoon garlic powder

1 tablespoon onion powder

1 teaspoon dried basil

1 teaspoon dried oregano

1 teaspoon dried thyme

1 teaspoon dried parsley flakes

1 teaspoon dried savory

1 teaspoon ground mace

1 teaspoon freshly ground black pepper

1 teaspoon dried sage

1 teaspoon dried marjoram

1 teaspoon ground dried grated lemon peel

Mix until well blended. Use as you would any seasoning salt.

MINT SAUCE FOR LAMB

4 sprigs of mint – leaves stripped

Castor sugar to sweeten (about 2 tablespoons)

Salt and pepper to taste

1/4 cup vinegar

3 tablespoons hot water

Cut mint leaves finely. Dissolve sugar in hot water, add mint leaves, vinegar, salt and pepper. Stir, crushing mint leaves against side of container as you go. (Use a mortar and pestle if you have one). Taste and adjust sugar to your taste.

FRESH MINT SALAD

3 handfuls of torn lettuce

½ red bell pepper finely sliced

1 Italian cucumber finely sliced

10 cherry tomatoes halved

12 shavings of tasty or parmesan cheese

3 tablespoons chopped parsley leaves

20 mint leaves torn in half

Toss together with Italian Dressing then on top dress with:

12 shavings of tasty or parmesan cheese

1 avocado sliced

John Dennan

HERBED FLAT BREAD (THE FAMILY FAVORITE)

Pre-heat oven to 425°F.

Heat oven trays before putting bread onto them.

3 flat bread or Lebanese bread

Lightly spread with garlic butter (4 cloves crushed garlic mixed with 6 tbs butter)

Sprinkle each flat bread with:

Mix of finely chopped: parsley, marjoram, oregano, basil

Chopped sundried tomatoes

Grated parmesan cheese

Small cubes of Philadelphia cheese

Put on hot tray and cook for approx. 10 minutes. Serve as a snack, with salad or with meals. To make this into a dinner pizza, just add more toppings.

SCRAMBLED EGGS

Lightly fry in pan:

1 tablespoon each of:

butter

red onion very finely chopped

parsley leaves

When onions are glassy add:

Whip very lightly together:

4 eggs

Pinch salt and pepper

1/2 cup of cream and/or milk (mixed is best)

Pour into pan. Let bottom layer cook then slowly push cooked mixture around allowing uncooked mixture to

John Dennan

bottom of pan. Gently continue this until all running mixture is cooked. Eggs should still look shiny when served. Serve with chopped chives and torn basil leaves on top and cut tomato on the side.

Extras could be toast, bacon and/or sausages.

To get the best scrambled eggs they need very light handling and not overcooking.

THE HERBAL MEDICINE CHART

Common herbs and what illnesses they can help.

Allspice	Mouthwash, pain relief
Basil (pregnant women avoid)	Tea for migraines. Douche for yeast infection.
Caraway	Relieves menstrual cramps, promotes menstruation
Cayenne Pepper	Relieves arthritis pain (can drop your sugar level)
Celery	Sedative, hypertension, kidneys
Chicory	Dissolves gallstones, cleans the liver
Cilantro	Prevents food poisoning
Clove	Toothaches, helps curb alcoholism
Dill	Insomnia
Fennel	Bad Breath
Garlic	Antibiotic
Ginger	Thins the blood
Oregano	Fever reducer
Mint	Heartburn, stomach aches
Nutmeg	Indigestion
Rosemary	Anti-oxidant
Sage	Insect bites, stings
Tarragon	Insomnia, depression
Thyme	Antibiotic
Turmeric	Anti-oxidant

CAUTION: Although these herbs are listed as helping with the ailments, any use should first be analyzed by your physician.

SUMMARY

There are many herbs growing all over the world. These versatile plants are used for everything from beautifying the garden to flavoring a meal. You will find herbs on drugstore shelves, listed as herbal remedies. There is no end to their use.

When you are in the garden, the anxiety and stress of the day seem to melt away. It is a time to relax and enjoy nature. The smell of the natural herbs wafting in the air is enough to make your mind wander too far off places. You can create an entire paradise with the herbs you plant in the garden.

Herbs do not need to be contained in one section of the garden, either. You can plant such herbs as echinacea and calendula right in the flower beds. Black cohosh makes a fantastic backdrop to some of the other flowering herbs.

What I love to do is have a pot of my most used herbs on the window sill in the kitchen. I always have parsley, basil and mint growing there. As I am an avid user of herbs these are not my only plants I also have them growing in the garden as well so that I am not restricted in my use of them.

It is a joy to be able to walk outside and pull off a sprig of mint to chew on, or clip fresh basil for a truly awesome pesto sauce. Knowing you have an entire spice shelf at your disposal can make you become a more creative chef. You may find certain herbs are just naturally able to blend together, such as cloves and cinnamon or rosemary and oregano.

As you become more familiar with the herbs and the flavors they can add to your dishes, you will become inclined to use them. You will also want to add some new varieties to the garden. Knowing there is an herb for every dish, even cakes and cookies can make you want to grow more of the aromatic plants.

John Dennan

You will find yourself looking forward to trying new recipes just to experiment with the herbs. The freshness in taste will show in every dish you create. You will be complimented on the blend of seasonings you have added.

Whether you decide to plant an herb garden for the simple joy of it or because you want to have the spices on hand, the effort will pay off. You can even pick the fresh herbs and dry them for gifts. There is no end to the creative ways herbs will influence your lifestyle.

ABOUT THE AUTHORS

John Dennan has been a keen gardener for many years and now that he is retired has taken to writing about his gardening experiences.

Much of this information is gleaned from his own experience but there is also a certain amount of information that has been resourced to ensure correct information.

Enjoy and grow well.

Kaye Dennan has been growing fresh herbs for many, many years both for home use and use in her food industry businesses. You will find endless tips in this book to help you have a healthy and fruitful herb garden of your choice.

John and Kaye have collaborated to share their knowledge so that you too can enjoy growing and using fresh herbs in your cooking and for medicinal purposes.

John Dennan

20834560R00049

Printed in Poland
by Amazon Fulfillment
Poland Sp. z o.o., Wrocław